HIDDEN PROFIT$

Stop Chasing Cash - Predictable Profit in 90 Days

DEBRA ANGILLETTA

HIDDEN PROFITS

"I hired my accountant to take care of the finances — someone to spot risks and guide strategy. But what I got was a Monday Morning Quarterback."

Dave, Business Owner

Table of Contents

7   **Introduction:** The Price Of Freedom

13   **Chapter 1:** Meet The Silent Partner That's Keeping You Broke

19   **Chapter 2:** Turn Your Financial Blindspots into a Cash Confidence Blueprint

23   **Chapter 3:** Why Your Accountant Isn't Driving Growth—The Fix That Transforms Your Business

27   **Chapter 4:** The Radical Shift: From Paper Profits to Money in the Bank

33   **Chapter 5:** The Power of Allocation–Break Free From Cash Flow Chaos (For Good!)

37   **Chapter 6:** Profits On Lock –The Money Move That Delivers Real Growth

41   **Chapter 7:** Hidden Expense Hit List – Why More Sales Won't Help (And What Actually Will)

47   **Chapter 8:** Outsmart Debt, Outpace Growth – How to Pay Down Debt and Keep Growing

55 **Chapter 9:** Escape Yesterday's Numbers–Unleash Your Power for Explosive Growth

59 **Chapter 10:** Financial Guidance–From Blind Decisions To a Sure Win

63 **Chapter 11:** What Could Have Been — The Cost of Missed Opportunity

67 **Chapter 12:** Long-Term Success Starts Here–Create a Business That Fuels Your Life

71 **Chapter 13:** From Barely Breaking Even to 10x Profits–Jennifer's Life Changing Moment

75 **Chapter 14:** The 90-Day Profit Plan – Crush Cash Chaos and Build Your Profit Machine

81 **Chapter 15:** Profit Next™ — Building a Profit-To-Wealth Blueprint

85 **Acknowledgements**

89 **About the Author**

Introduction:
The Price of Freedom

Growing up, money wasn't a tool. It was a weapon. It didn't serve joy, peace, or connection. It ruled. Quietly and completely. It shaped who spoke, who stayed silent, what dreams were dared, and what moments were missed.

In my house, money wasn't a servant. It was the master.

My father was a brilliant man. Valedictorian of the School of Hard Knocks. Technically gifted. Sharp-witted. A contagious laugh. But beneath it all, he was broken. I often think of him as a misguided Jedi. Someone with incredible potential, but pulled toward darkness by grief.

He lost his mother at an age when he needed her most, and his father, already shattered by the loss of a daughter, had no room left in his heart for another child. My dad never stood a chance. Rejection like that doesn't fade. It brands you for life.

He worked tirelessly. Often on call, sometimes through snowstorms in the dead of night, maintaining complex hardware systems for Honeywell. The job paid well, but the cost was time, presence, and peace. He always came home tired and completely miserable.

Along the way, my father inherited two homes from his family. Small, older properties tucked away in neighborhoods that had seen better days. Rather than sell or renovate, he chose to become a low-income housing landlord. It wasn't a calling. It was a calculation.

He never wanted to fix anything. Not properly, anyway. He patched things up in the cheapest way possible, if at all. After he died, we found a toilet he'd jerry-rigged with a necklace—one he'd found in a mall parking lot. It was so on-brand for him, it almost felt like a final message. The basement of my childhood home would flood anytime a freak rainstorm passed through. He knew the foundation needed work. He just wouldn't spend the money to fix it.

To him, money meant: give as little as possible, take as much as you can. Invest, but never improve. I wish he could have realized how he treated money, that if you trap it, hoard it, starve it, it suffocates. And everything around it suffocates with it. Control the resource, control the people.

That mindset didn't stop there. It seeped into our home. Into his marriage.

My mother saw money differently. For her, it wasn't a source of power. It was a source of possibility. While my father worked, my mother managed the burden of the rentals. She fielded tenant complaints, chased down overdue rent, and handled the upkeep. But she saw more than rundown rentals; she saw potential. With some repairs, fresh paint, and thoughtful remodeling, she believed the homes could attract better tenants and command higher rents.

One day, my mother asked my father to add her name to the rental deeds. A sign of partnership. A nod to her effort.

They scheduled a meeting with an attorney. But that morning, just before the signing, my father backed out.

"I can't do this," he said.

My mother looked at him steadily and clearly. "Then I can't do this either."

My father feared losing control over money more than anything. Because in his heart, it was never about the money, it was the last fragile thread connecting him to the mother he lost at age 13. She had been a sharp, forward-thinking investor in the 1950s, often taking my dad with her to company shareholder meetings. The estate she left him was her final whisper. And he guarded it with the intensity of a son who never stopped missing her, protecting it with an unwavering, almost desperate devotion.

To that end, the man who maintained machines couldn't maintain his marriage.

He never lost money, but in the end, he lost everything.

He lost his family. My mother filed for divorce.

After becoming a single-parent household, we were no longer doing well. We were doing okay. There was food, clothes, and a roof over our heads. But a slim margin for anything extra.

And then came **the jeans.**

In middle school, Jordache jeans were everything. A symbol of status, acceptance, and cool. Every girl had them. Some had two pairs. My classmate, Joanne Kaiser, I swear, had ten!

I had **none.**

My mom, doing the best she could, bought me a knockoff pair of designer jeans from Sears. They tried to pass for Jordache but fooled no one. They fit terribly. If you weren't shaped like a pencil, they gapped at the waist and bunched at the ankles. I hated them. I wore them like a scarlet letter…an announcement that I didn't belong.

That was my moment. A silent vow burned inside of me:

Never again.

Never again would I feel that shame. Never again would I **depend on someone else's wallet.** As a teenager, I realized that if I earned my own money, I could buy what I wanted, even when my mom couldn't. That was the moment I tasted financial independence for the first time.

And yes, eventually I bought that coveted pair of Jordache jeans.

Funny enough, the joke was on me, because those jeans fit just as terribly as the Sears knockoffs.

But it wasn't about the jeans. It was about choice, and the power to buy them myself.

That's when I realized: if I wanted real freedom, I couldn't just make money, I had to understand it.

That was the spark.

I fell in love with finance. Not for the spreadsheets, but the liberation. When you understand money, you don't hide from bills or balances. You walk toward them, head high, pen ready. You create your own possibility.

That lesson deepened the summer when I turned fifteen.

My father had promised to take us to Disney. It would be our first time. I was not exactly the age when fairytales still held their magic, but old enough to know when something special was being offered. My younger brother, though, was still in that wide-eyed stage. The trip was really for him.

We were giddy, making lists of the rides, roller coasters, and firework displays. My brother had never been on a plane. The trip was magic in the making.

I believe my father had the best of intentions. But old habits die hard.

Soon after, my dad had started seeing someone new, a woman with a young daughter who had special needs. They were offered an all-expenses-paid trip to Disney through some family program. Instead of figuring out how to bring us, or even rescheduling the trip he had promised, he agreed to go with them.

He said yes to a free trip to Disney.

And we were left behind.

Mom never raged. But something broke in her that day. And in its place, a quiet determination formed.

A week later, she came home, purse still on her shoulder, and called us into the living room.

"Guess what?" she said. "We're going to Disney."

I blinked. "Where did you get the money for that?"

She smiled. "A really good tax refund."

The truth? There was no tax refund.

I believed that lie for decades.

She used her savings—scraped together from a job that paid $15,000 a year and child support checks of $80 a week. In 1987, that was just enough to get by. But she used it to heal our broken hearts.

She bought the plane tickets. The hotel. The park passes. She even brought my grandmother so the memory could stretch across three generations.

It was the only time I have ever been to Disney.

But it was enough.

It was everything.

Because it wasn't just about the trip, it was about **choice**. About showing us that money could create magic, not just misery.

I've lived on both sides of money. One parent clutched it like oxygen. The other let it breathe, and through that generosity, created miracles.

Both shaped me. My money story became my greatest gift, and I'm grateful to both of my parents for playing exactly the roles they were meant to play.

I understand my father's fear. I've lived my mother's faith. I know how easy it is to let money define your worth, your voice, your future, even when you think you're the one in control.

But then I remember my father, where money was his master and fear ruled his every decision. And then I remember my mother. And I remember Disney. And I remember that money, when used with intention, can be a powerful servant. A healer. A source of freedom.

Sometimes I still fall into those negative thought patterns around money as a business owner, whispering fear and scarcity. In those moments, I return to the work, the sacred practice that brings me back to the truth — the abundance, the freedom.

Real wealth isn't a brand name, a fancy car, or a bank balance, it's the power to choose.

Those knockoff jeans gave me more than middle school humiliation. Now, as a business owner, they gave me a mission.

I wrote this book for you, the business owner tired of feeling trapped by money's rules and ready to rewrite them. For the entrepreneur who wants more than just survival or getting by. This book is your roadmap to understanding your finances on your terms, to turning money from a source of stress into a source of freedom and choice.

Because I believe that when you take charge of your money, your mindset, and business, it means you're turning your grind into building wealth that changes lives, starting with your own.

And that's the real ticket to freedom.

Chapter 1:
Meet The Silent Partner That's Keeping You Broke

I interviewed over one hundred business owners as research for this book.

Many business owners often described their accountants as a silent partner.

They're there in the background, keeping the books tidy and the taxes filed, but something critical is missing: **active engagement**.

While accurate record-keeping is essential, many entrepreneurs feel their accounting professionals fail to partner in their success.

After interviewing hundreds of active and engaged entrepreneurs, the complaint is universal:

> *"I only hear from my accountant when it's tax time, everything else is radio silence."*

But what about the other times? When a business owner is navigating cash flow issues, debating an investment decision, or considering expansion?

These aren't just moments of financial housekeeping. These are **fork-in-the-road decisions** that require more than historical data; they demand foresight, advice, and actionable insight.

The Reality Behind the Role

Accountants are trained and rewarded for compliance, ensuring that documentation is captured and forms are filed on time. That's important. But most entrepreneurs are looking for more.

You want insight.
You want visibility.
You want to know if there's enough for the priorities that matter—**profit, payroll, taxes, growth, and peace of mind**.

The role of an accountant should go beyond compliance. Yet, for many, that's where the service ends.

This isn't just frustrating for business owners, it's **costly**.

Missed opportunities, inefficient spending, and reactive financial decisions don't come from bad bookkeeping.

They come from a lack of proactive guidance.

Why Accounting Professionals Remain Reactive

Understanding the problem helps you avoid falling victim to it. Here's what's going on behind the scenes.

1. Lack of Training

Most accountants are educated in compliance and tax law, not cash flow. They know how to track what happened, not how to advise on what's next. Forecasting, financial strategy, and profitability planning often fall outside their area of expertise.

Example: A business owner faces ongoing cash flow issues. Her accountant provides accurate financial statements but offers no strategic recommendations to improve margins or restructure expenses. The result? The cycle continues.

2. Time Constraints

Accountants are stretched thin, managing compliance tasks for dozens or even hundreds of clients. Their time is consumed by urgent deadlines, leaving no room for proactive financial coaching.

Example: A growing tech firm asks its accountant for help evaluating expansion options. Instead, they get a delayed response, months later, because the accountant was buried in tax season.

3. Mindset and Willingness

Some accountants don't see strategic guidance as part of their job. Others worry that offering advice might lead to blame if results go sideways. So, they stay quiet, even when they see something that could help.

Silent Partner Problem

Meet **Samantha**, a smart, capable entrepreneur who runs a digital marketing agency. She brings in consistent revenue and works with an accountant who sends her neat monthly reports.

One month, the numbers reveal a troubling trend: profits are shrinking, even as revenue rises.

Her accountant notices the issue. He suspects rising contractor costs and unchecked software subscriptions are draining cash. But he tells himself:

> *"It's not really my place to suggest what she should cut back on. I'm just here to keep the books clean. If I speak up and she acts on it—and it doesn't work out—it could backfire."*

So… he says nothing.

And Samantha, assuming things are under control, keeps moving forward. Months go by. The problem worsens. She eventually takes out a loan to cover payroll, when a few early adjustments could have preserved her profits and avoided unnecessary debt.

Samantha's story is all too common, but it doesn't have to end that way.

It's what business owners are calling the **Silent Partner Problem**: your accountant is tracking the score, but no one is helping you lead the game.

Cash Protector

The first step out of this trap is to shift from *rearview reports* to *forward-looking visibility*. A simple mechanism I use with clients is a **Cash Protector - a two-question approval process**.

Once a month, ask two questions before approving expenses:

1. Does this expense directly help us generate or protect revenue?

2. Could this be delayed, reduced, or replaced?

This small shift gives you control rather than blind trust in reports.

Try this today: open your bank statement and circle your top three recurring subscriptions. Cancel or downgrade one that isn't tied to growth. That one small step can immediately lift your margin, and more importantly, give you momentum.

I've seen clients add back 5–10% profit in the first 30 days by running these profit checkpoints. They didn't need to sell more, just tighten up what was quietly draining cash.

Samantha didn't have this framework, but now you will.

Closing Summary

You don't have to settle for an accountant who simply keeps score. You need a real system, one that gives you clarity, confidence, and doesn't make you want to fake your own disappearance every tax season.

The silent partner model is broken.

Next, we'll uncover the sneaky little blind spots that are draining your profits and the subtle ways they're holding your business back, sometimes without you even knowing it. Let's bring those into the light, so you can stop guessing, start leading, and finally build a business that pays you back.

FREE GIFT:
The 5 Questions to Ask
Your Accountant Every Month

If you want better answers, you need better questions. Start here.
Your accountant gives you history, not clarity, which is why running your business feels like driving with the headlights off.
This tool fixes that in five minutes. You'll get the five questions that instantly reveal where your money went, what's about to break, and what you must focus on to increase profit this month. No jargon. No spreadsheets. Just five questions that tell you the truth.

You can check it out at findmyhiddenprofits.com/tools
or scan the QR code for ease.

Chapter 2

Turn Your Financial Blind Spots into a Cash Confidence Blueprint

Last year, Nicole, a successful event planner, scrambled for cash during an unusually slow season. Clients were delaying deposits, costs were rising, and cash flow had dried up fast.

She turned to her accountant for help.

Instead of offering strategic suggestions or analyzing trends to help her find opportunities, the accountant handed over last quarter's financial statements. A table full of numbers. No guidance. No plan. Just the expectation that Nicole would somehow find clarity on her own.

With no actionable insight and no time to spare, she did what many business owners do, she quickly decided under pressure. She opened a high-interest credit line to float her expenses. When business picked up again, she wasn't relieved, she was buried in repayments. That one desperate choice created a ripple effect that would follow her for years.

Nicole's story is painful, but it's also **preventable**.

Decisions In The Dark

Business owners stated that their daily lives consisted of juggling everything—from sales, marketing, hiring, delivery, and administration. You shouldn't also have to be a finance expert. But when your accountant is focused only on tax deadlines and basic bookkeeping, you're left trying to make decisions in the dark.

And decisions made in the dark are almost always expensive.

Every time you ask for advice about increasing profits, making a hire, or managing cash, you're met with a blank stare, or a spreadsheet with no explanation.

You're not crazy for feeling like you're alone in it.

You are.

The Real Cost of Financial Blind Spots

This gap, this blind spot in strategic financial direction, comes with consequences:

- You overextend during slow seasons
- You hesitate on investments that could accelerate growth
- You waste money on subscriptions or vendors that aren't adding value
- You avoid hiring (or hire the wrong person) because you're unsure what you can afford
- You default to emotion instead of clarity when making spending decisions

And worse? When life hits, an unexpected lawsuit, illness, divorce, staff turnover, or market disruption, you don't have the reserves or structure in place to absorb the shock.

It's not because you're careless.

It's because no one gave you a better way.

Cash Confidence Blueprint

Here's the good news: you don't need a finance degree to run a profitable, healthy business. You need **a simple system for visibility and control**.

I call it the **Cash Confidence Blueprint**—a method that:

- Shows you exactly where your money is going
- Helps you course-correct in real time
- Gives you the confidence to invest, hire, and grow without fear

This framework takes you beyond spreadsheets, replacing blind spots with clear, actionable insight.

Fix the Cash Timing Gap

Nicole didn't have a revenue problem, she had a **cash-timing problem.** The fastest way to avoid her mistake is to fix that gap.

Here's how:

- **Tighten client payment terms**: Require upfront deposits or milestone payments (e.g., 50% upfront, 50% at completion).
- **Negotiate vendor terms**: Ask for 30–60 day terms so your outflows align with inflows.
- **Offer early-payment incentives**: Give small discounts to clients who pay faster.

Any of these steps can ease cash strain almost immediately. Together, they turn survival mode into breathing room.

What Happens When You Do This

One of my clients, a marketing agency owner, shifted just two contracts to upfront deposits and saved herself over $40,000 in interest payments that year. She didn't increase sales, she improved timing. That's the power of visibility.

Closing Summary

When you don't have a clear financial picture, even good decisions can become risky, and bad ones become expensive.

Your accountant's job is to report the past. Super helpful...if you're building a time machine.

But your job as CEO **is to lead into the future.**

To do that, you need more than clean books—you need a framework that gives you clarity before crisis strikes.

In the next chapter, I'll walk you through the next step so you can start eliminating blind spots and building a business that supports you rather than stresses you out.

FREE GIFT:
The Cash Timing Snapshot

Your cash isn't broken, your timing is. This tool shows exactly when money shows up, when bills strike, and how to fix the gap instantly: Cash in early. Bills out later. Fast. Simple. Stress-reducing. No math. No spreadsheets. Just clarity you can act on today.

Get it at <u>findmyhiddenprofits.com/tools</u>
or scan the QR code if your phone deserves to feel useful today.

Chapter 3:

Why Your Accountant Isn't Driving Growth—The Fix That Transforms Your Business

During my research interviews for this book, business owners consistently expressed a strong desire for their accountants to be more than just number crunchers, they want a trusted partner who helps them navigate challenges and uncover new opportunities.

The Cost of Assumptions

After years of grinding, Liam finally hit his stride. His eco-friendly e-commerce brand took off, sales surged, and he reinvested all proceeds into inventory. His revenue numbers looked incredible, so he assumed profit was keeping pace.

And why wouldn't he? He had an accountant.

His thinking? *"If something wasn't working... they'd tell me, right?"*

Wrong.

No one ever sat down with Liam to analyze his margins. No one stress-tested his growth plan. His accountant was focused on taxes and compliance, not strategy.

By the time Liam realized the truth, it was too late. His bestsellers were losing money after fees and shipping. He was sitting on piles of unsold stock, behind on payroll, and drowning under a high-interest loan.

All because he thought compliance was the same thing as strategy.

The Emotional Cost

If your accountant only files taxes and reconciles books, you're left on your own to make the decisions that determine whether your business thrives or collapses.

And that takes a toll.

- You're constantly second-guessing yourself.
- You're stuck reacting instead of planning.
- You feel like you're missing opportunities but can't pinpoint where.

It's exhausting. Because deep down, you don't just want someone to do the books, you want a partner who helps you *win the game.*

What's at Stake

Missed opportunities don't just cost money, they cost momentum, confidence, and sometimes years of progress.

Liam's story is the perfect example:

- **Money left on the table:** ~$20,000 in potential net profit lost
- **Money wasted:** $8,000+ in fees and high-interest debt
- **Opportunity cost:** A six-month growth delay

That's not just bookkeeping, it's the difference between scaling a thriving business and stalling out.

Compliance vs. Strategy

Let's be clear: your accountant is important. Taxes and compliance matter. But that's the foundation.

Most business owners need a **strategic advisor**—someone who goes beyond reporting the past to help you create the future.

This is not about firing your accountant. It's about adding the missing piece.

Think of it like building a Formula 1 team:

- Your accountant is the mechanic, essential for keeping the engine running.

- Your strategic advisor is the race strategist, reading the track ahead, timing the pit stops, and helping you win.

Both roles matter. But only one drives growth.

What the Right Advisor Does for You

When you bring in the right strategic partner, you:

- Spot and stop profit leaks before they drain you
- Plan proactively instead of reacting to crises
- Create safety nets with reserves and smart structures
- Make confident choices about pricing, hiring, and scaling
- Align money decisions with your long-term goals

This is how you escape the cycle of what could have been and start building the wins waiting for you.

Closing Summary

You don't need to settle for a financial partner who only looks backward.

You don't need to keep wondering what opportunities you're missing.

You deserve a **financial ally**—someone who brings clarity, control, and confidence to every decision you make.

When you add the right strategic advisor alongside your accountant, you:

- Stop guessing

- Start leading with intention

- Build a business that grows profitably and sustainably

The cost of staying stuck in compliance-only support is high. But the payoff of making the shift? It transforms everything.

Because growth isn't about who files your taxes. It's about who's in your corner when the stakes are highest.

Your business is built for speed. Now it's time to assemble the pit crew built to keep up.

FREE GIFT:
The Advisor Scorecard

Your "financial support" might be costing you growth.
This scorecard shows—fast—whether your advisor can spot problems early, guide strategic decisions, and actually help you scale...
or if they're just reporting the past while you're trying to build a future.
One minute. One score. All truth.

Grab it at findmyhiddenprofits.com/tools
or scan the QR code if you dread typing.

Chapter 4:
The Radical Shift: From Paper Profits to Money in the Bank

After decades advising hundreds of business owners since I started my career in wealth and finance back in 1988, I've noticed a powerful pattern.

As a business owner, you're probably used to the traditional way of managing finances, where you pay your expenses first and then hope there's something left over for profit.

Because you love your business and the impact it has, you keep coming last and will even forgo a paycheck if it means the business can keep going.

The problem with this approach is that profit becomes an afterthought, rather than a priority. It's easy to get stuck in a cycle of running on thin margins, constantly worrying about how to make ends meet.

Feeling the reward of business ownership, after all, you took all the risk, you had the vision, you've been the one juggling all the priorities. You deserve to be well compensated because your business is performing well, and you deserve to feel secure as you grow it.

Flipping The Script

Sustainable businesses aren't built on emotional decisions or trying to keep the IRS happy.

Real businesses use real strategies to be financially successful.

Flip the script by making profits the first thing you set aside, ensuring that your business becomes sustainable from the start, not just when the numbers work out at the end of the year.

By focusing on profits, you're setting your business up for long-term success. When profit is treated as a fixed expense — like taxes or payroll — it forces you to be disciplined about spending, reducing the emotional stress of financial uncertainty.

The businesses that grow sustainably, that scale without burning out, that actually reward their owners, do one thing differently.

They make **profit non-negotiable**.

When I discovered the book **Profit First** by Mike Michalowicz through a colleague, it hit me like a lightning bolt. For the first time, there was a simple, practical framework that forces businesses to pay themselves first. Not when there's money left over. Not after taxes and payroll. But profit—first.

And the businesses that implement it?

They don't just survive. They thrive.

The Emotional Cost

Here's the hard truth: most business owners live on paper profits.

On paper, the P&L says you're profitable. But in your bank account? Crickets.

That disconnect leaves you:

- Scrambling to cover payroll even though revenue looks strong

- Forgoing your own paycheck just to keep things going

- Stuck in financial anxiety, wondering where the money went

It's heartbreaking. You took the risks. You made the sacrifices. You work long hours. But when it comes time to be rewarded, you're the one left waiting.

That cycle isn't just stressful, it's unsustainable.

What's at Stake

When profit is an afterthought, you miss:

- The ability to build a true emergency fund

- The chance to invest in opportunities without going into debt

- The security of knowing you're paid consistently, like any other member of your team

Profit isn't just extra money. It's the engine that fuels growth, stability, and peace of mind.

Without it, you're stuck in the cycle of hustle and hope.

From Hope to Certainty

Here's the radical shift: stop treating profit like a leftover. Treat it like a fixed expense.

That's the brilliance of Profit First.

It forces you to carve out profit before you spend, which changes the entire way you run your business.

Think about it:

- Taxes are non-negotiable.
- Payroll is non-negotiable.
- Why shouldn't profit be the same?

When you move profit to the front of the line, you no longer let cash flow control you. **You control it.**

What the Right System Does for You

With Profit First, you:

- Pay yourself consistently, reaping the rewards of ownership
- Build a profit buffer that doubles as an emergency fund
- Eliminate the stress of surprise tax bills
- Gain clarity with real dollars in dedicated accounts, not abstract numbers on a spreadsheet

And most importantly? You start to believe again.

You see that your business isn't just capable of generating revenue, it's capable of generating wealth.

Make It Real

Open **three new bank accounts today**:

1. **Profit Account** – Your reward for the risk and vision you bring to the table

2. **Owner's Compensation Account** – Your consistent paycheck as the leader

3. **Tax Account** – A buffer so tax season never blindsides you again

Start by moving a small percentage of every deposit into each account. Watch how quickly you feel the shift—clarity, confidence, and control, all from a simple system.

Closing Summary

Profit isn't a bonus. It's the foundation.

Profit First turns paper profits into real money in the bank.

This isn't just a financial system, it's a mindset shift that transforms the way you run your business and the way you experience your life as an owner.

Because the truth is: you didn't build your business to keep the lights on. You built it for freedom, impact, and a return on the sweat you've poured into it.

And it starts by paying yourself first.

Now that you've embraced profit as non-negotiable, the next step is mastering the flow of money in and out.

In the next chapter, we'll dive into your **Cash Allocation Engine** that kills the stress, eliminates nasty surprises, and keeps your business humming like your favorite Friday night playlist.

Chapter 5:
The Power of Allocation– Break Free From Cash Flow Chaos (For Good!)

Imagine this: it's the 28th of the month. Your bills are due. You just got paid, but somehow the numbers don't add up. You're sweating, scrolling through spreadsheets, wondering if you can pay yourself, your team, and the landlord without going over funds in your account. Sound familiar?

Even profitable business owners feel trapped like this. Money comes in, money goes out, and you're left wondering, "Where did it all go?" The chaos steals your focus, your sleep, and your confidence.

You're profitable on paper, but your bank account screams a different story.

Welcome to cash flow chaos. It's exhausting.

This chapter will guide you step-by-step through creating a framework customized for your business, freeing you from financial chaos and giving you peace of mind that every dollar is working toward your success.

Feeling trapped by cash flow chaos is one of the most exhausting parts of running a business. You work hard, make sacrifices, and yet, somehow, the money just never seems to land where it should, leaving you stressed, scrambling, and stuck on a financial treadmill you can't escape.

But what if you could break free?

What if the cycle of uncertainty, last-minute scrambles, and cash flow headaches didn't have to be your story anymore?

This chapter shows you how the power of smart money allocation can untangle that chaos, give you clarity, and put you back in the driver's seat of your business finances, for good.

Alicia's Story

Alicia is an attorney with her own practice, making $20,000/month. Some months, she paid herself last, hoping there would be enough after bills, payroll, and taxes. Spoiler: some months there weren't. She'd stress over late invoices, scramble to cover vendor payments, and lie awake at night wondering if she'd miscalculated again.

That constant juggling, the fear of running short, the what-ifs, it's mentally draining and keeps you from growing the business you worked so hard to build.

Now, picture a different reality. One where every dollar has a job. Every account is clear. Bills get paid. Taxes are covered. You get paid. Profit actually grows.

This is the power of allocation. By dividing revenue into clear categories—Profit, Owner's Pay, Taxes, Operating Expenses—you turn chaos into clarity. You stop reacting to your money and start leading it.

Cash Allocation Engine

Alicia set up four accounts and allocated her $20,000/month like this:

- **Profit:** 5% → $1,000
- **Owner's Pay:** 50% → $10,000
- **Taxes:** 15% → $3,000
- **Operating Expenses:** 30% → $6,000

The result? Instant clarity. She saw exactly where her money was going, caught overspending on office expenses, finally paid herself consistently, and watched her profit grow. No more scrambling. No more panic. Pure confidence.

Allocation isn't complicated. It's intentional. Every dollar is assigned a purpose before it touches your hands. It fosters discipline, prevents overspending, and empowers you to make data-driven decisions, not stress-driven ones.

Start Your Cash Allocation Engine Today

1. Open dedicated accounts for Profit, Owner's Pay, Taxes, and Operating Expenses.

2. Decide allocation percentages that fit your revenue and goals.

3. Every time money comes in, immediately distribute it according to your plan.

4. Monitor, tweak, and watch the chaos disappear.

Closing Summary

Cash flow chaos doesn't have to be your story. With an allocation engine, you reclaim control.

You see the money, direct the money, and make your business work for you, not the other way around.

By adopting a clear, consistent allocation engine, you're not just protecting your profit, you're drawing a money map that leads straight to smarter spending, sharper decisions, and growth that sticks around longer than a New Year's resolution.

Quick heads up: no one nails this perfectly on day one, but it's about taking that first step and building a habit that puts you back in the driver's seat.

Start small, keep it steady, and watch this radical shift flip your financial script.

Cash flow chaos? Consider it officially evicted.

Your profitable future? It's moving in — and redecorating the place.

An allocation engine solves the chaos. But if you stop here, there's still a trap: treating profit as optional instead of required.

In the next chapter, we'll raise the stakes: how to place **Profit On Lock.**

Because when profit is locked in first, before a single dollar goes anywhere else, your mindset shifts, your habits change, and growth becomes real, not just theoretical.

FREE GIFT:
Clearing The Cash Constraint

A simple one-page map that shows exactly where your money flows, and where it gets stuck. In 2 minutes, you'll see why cash feels tight, what's leaking, and the one fix that gives you instant relief.
No math. No percentages. Just clarity.

Grab it at <u>findmyhiddenprofits.com/tools</u>
or scan the QR code if you're allergic to extra steps.

Chapter 6:
Profits On Lock – The Money Move That Delivers Real Growth

When I start working with business owners who are already familiar with the Profit First system (often through reading the book), they are often overwhelmed and tense about whether they are doing it correctly.

They're given a table and instructions passively, and do their best to implement, but as busy entrepreneurs, **they often struggle to fully adopt the system.**

This tension causes them to underspend in important categories or continue making stressful financial decisions (the worst kind!) because, although they have more visibility, they aren't forecasting or seeing the ripple effects of their financial choices.

Many entrepreneurs don't follow the system exactly. Instead, they try to overlay the principles from the book onto the old processes or skip the analysis needed to find their ideal allocation targets. This only creates more chaos and guilt.

Profit Comes First

Most business owners treat profit like a wish, not a rule. Pay bills, cover expenses, hope something's left. That mindset leads to stress, financial insecurity, and constant second-guessing.

When you prioritize profit from the start, you begin to shift your entire mindset about your business's financial health. It's a commitment to making your business a success from the beginning, not something you hope happens at the end of the year.

Once you start your cash allocation engine, you'll notice that your spending habits change. Instead of spending everything on day-to-day operations and leaving nothing for profit, you think more strategically about how to allocate your funds.

This approach also helps you avoid the temptation to overspend. Each decision becomes more intentional because you've already committed to paying yourself and saving for profit. Over time, this will reduce financial stress and help you build a solid, profitable foundation for your business.

Reflect on your current mindset about profits and finances. Ask yourself: Is profit truly a priority, or just something you hope will happen?

Small Start, Big Impact

Start small. Pick a profit percentage—1%, 5%, whatever works, and **set that money aside first, every time revenue comes in**. **Every. Single. Transaction.**

Lock it in. Start small. Stay consistent.

Watch how your habits, mindset, and growth shift.

That simple habit builds momentum, reshapes your thinking, and puts you back in control of your business finances right away.

Remember, small consistent steps build momentum. Over time, this commitment grows your confidence, reduces financial stress, and builds a healthier, more profitable business foundation.

This approach helps mitigate the chaos and guilt that come from unmanaged finances by providing a clear, structured way to prioritize profit. This ensures your business grows based on real profits, not borrowed funds or wishful thinking.

When profits are on lock, profitability becomes inevitable.

Closing Summary

Many entrepreneurs struggle because they try to apply these principles to old habits, skipping analysis or allocation. That creates stress and chaos. But with a partner who guides you through full implementation, profit-first thinking becomes real. Businesses start protecting profit, making smarter moves, and seeing tangible growth. Stress drops, confidence rises, and finances finally make sense.

Profits on lock isn't just some fancy finance trick, it's a mindset makeover that flips how you run your whole business. When you put profit first, you clear the runway for real growth, financial security, and that sweet, sweet peace of mind.

Start small, stay consistent, and build momentum until your business is practically doing backflips.

Profit is your well-deserved trophy for all the risks and hustle you've thrown down. Lock it in, and your business won't just survive, it'll thrive, turning your big dreams into a sustainable success story.

Act today to make profit your new BFF. This money move is the game-changer your business has been waiting for.

In the next chapter, we'll reveal the **Hidden Expense Hit List**—why more revenue without disciplined spending can swallow your gains—and show exactly how to protect profit while scaling smarter.

Get ready to break free from the myth that sales equal success, and

learn what actually moves the needle for your business.

FREE GIFT:
The Profits-On-Lock Tracker

Make profit automatic—every deposit, every time. Most owners mean to put profit first…but life gets busy and it slips. This one-page tracker fixes that. Pick your percentage, check off each transfer, and watch profit become a habit, not a hope. Use it for 30 days and see both your confidence and your cash grow.

Get it at <u>findmyhiddenprofits.com/tools</u>
or scan the QR code if convenience is your love language.

Chapter 7:
Hidden Expense Hit List – Why More Sales Won't Help (And What Actually Will)

You've taken a huge step by making profit non-negotiable, shifting your mindset and your money management in a way that sets your business up for real growth and stability. But here's a truth many business owners don't realize:

More sales alone won't fix your financial struggles.

If you've been chasing more sales, believing that revenue automatically equals bigger profits and freedom, it's time for a reality check.

More sales sound like growth, right? But without controlling expenses, more revenue can actually **deepen your financial struggles**. Welcome to the Expense Trap: the cycle where higher sales lead to rising costs, squeezing your profits tighter and tighter, until you're stressed, stuck, and wondering why all your hard work isn't paying off.

The truth: growth without control is a double-edged sword. Money comes in, but it **quickly disappears** into unexpected expenses, poor spending decisions, or overinvestment in the wrong areas.

In this chapter, you'll learn:

- Why more sales can sometimes hurt your bottom line
- How to spot the Expense Trap before it traps you
- The strategic moves that protect your profits and fuel sustainable growth

Finding Your Partner In Profit

Let's be clear: your bookkeeper and accountant aren't scanning your expenses for leaks, waste, or hidden opportunities. It's not that they're bad at their job, **it's just not their job.**

They focus on accuracy and compliance, including proper categorization and timely tax filings. **That's different from financial strategy. That's different from profit recovery. That's different from building wealth.**

Here's the game-changer: I dig deep into your operating expenses to find the **money slipping through the cracks**. Line by line. Not because I love spreadsheets (well… maybe a little), but because **that's where the hidden profits live**.

The fastest way to increase profitability? **Keep more of what you already earn.** Plug the silent leaks draining your margins. I've uncovered millions in hidden profits for clients—six- and seven-figure businesses that were bleeding cash without even realizing they were losing it.

Case Study: The $274,000 Wake-Up Call

Lisa runs a successful corporate training company. On paper, everything looked great: multi-six-figure revenue, a talented team, consistent client flow. But she came to me because something didn't feel right.

"I'm working non-stop, but there's never enough left over," she told me. "Where's the money going?"

That's the million-dollar question, and one your accountant isn't asking.

We dug in: line by line, no fluff. Here's what we found:

- $1,800/month in overlapping software tools no one used

- A marketing agency on retainer delivering zero qualified leads for 4 months

- Team roles drifting into vague, low-return, busy work

- Office lease costing $5,000/month while the team worked remotely

- Auto-renewing memberships, agency fees, and subscriptions she hadn't touched in a year

Total: $274,000 wasted in 12 months.

No major layoffs. No sacrificing growth. Just **smart cash reallocation.**

Within the next quarter, Lisa:

- Increased her pay

- Rebuilt her cash reserve

- Hired a strategic operations lead

Revenue went **up** because she finally had clarity and breathing room to focus on growth.

This result isn't an outlier. Profit doesn't hide, it just waits for someone to look closer.

Hidden Expense Hit List - Free Cash in 30 Days:

1. **Software Subscriptions (SaaS Creep)** – Unused, duplicate, or legacy tools

2. **Overstaffing/Poor Role Alignment** – Roles without measurable ROI

3. **Marketing Without Metrics** – Spending without tracking results

4. **Office Space & Utilities** – Paying for unused or unnecessary space

5. **Professional Services on Autopilot** – Retainers with unclear value

6. **Unmanaged Travel & Entertainment** – Loose policies creating bloated costs

7. **Inventory/Supplies Overload** – Tying up cash in slow-moving items

8. **High Merchant Processing Fees** – Overpaying for payment processing

9. **Outsourcing Without Oversight** – Paying without accountability

10. **Recurring Set & Forget Charges** – Auto-renewals you forgot about

Audit, cancel, consolidate, and align expenses with results. Small changes can unlock huge cash flow and profit potential.

Keep More, Grow More

Imagine reclaiming just 5–10% of operational spend. That's money for:

- Increasing your pay
- Funding strategic hires
- Fueling your next big investment

Profit isn't about selling more, it's about **keeping more**.

More profit doesn't come from more hustle, it comes from smarter moves.

Stop letting expenses silently drain your growth.

Plug the leaks. Reallocate. Watch your margins soar.

Closing Summary

No matter how much revenue you bring in, unchecked expenses can sneakily drain your profits faster than your coffee disappears on a Monday morning, and quietly hold your business back. Your bookkeeper and accountant? Total rock stars at keeping your books accurate and compliant. But the critical job of **spotting hidden leaks and optimizing spending**? That often gets lost in the shuffle.

By being intentional about finding and fixing these hidden expenses, you take control of your cash and **unlock serious profit potential**. Small changes—like canceling unused subscriptions, matching roles to actual results, or scrutinizing marketing spend—can add up to massive improvements. Ask Lisa, who went from "Where'd my money go?!" to "Show me the profits!"

Remember, **profit isn't just about selling more; it's about keeping more.**

The secret to long-term financial health? Make your **Hidden Expense Hit List** your obsession. Keep reviewing, keep questioning ("Seriously, do we need this?"), and keep reallocating like a boss. Your business will thank you with growth so solid that even your accountant will be impressed.

Now that you know how expenses quietly drain profits, it's time to **tackle the other side of the profit equation: debt**.

Next, we'll explore how to **Outsmart Debt and Outpace Growth**—a system for paying down debt strategically, taking control of cash flow, and positioning your business to grow profitably without unnecessary stress.

You've learned how to **keep more of what you earn**—now, you'll learn how to **use what you keep to gain momentum, crush debt, and accelerate growth.**

FREE GIFT:
The Hidden Expense Finder

Find the money you didn't know you were losing, and reclaim it fast. More sales won't fix cash stress if expenses are quietly leaking profit. This 5-minute tool exposes the biggest drains and shows you where to cut first. You'll get a 10-item checklist, a simple score to spot your biggest leaks, and one fast action to free up cash immediately. No spreadsheets. No overwhelm. Just found money.

Grab yours at <u>findmyhiddenprofits.com/tools</u> or scan the QR code. Consider it your smart financial decision for the day.

Chapter 8

Outsmart Debt, Outpace Growth – How to Pay Down Debt and Keep Growing

You've worked hard to build your business, but there's a catch: profits can disappear faster than you think, not just from low sales, but from hidden drains on your cash. Missed opportunities, creeping expenses, and lingering debt can make growth feel impossible.

Imagine if you could take control of your profits, pay down debt strategically, and still invest in the growth your business deserves. You can, and it starts with a clear plan.

Why Debt Feels Like a Trap

Debt can feel like a heavy backpack you carry everywhere. Some debts quietly strangle your cash flow; others tempt you with quick fixes and flashy promises. Many business owners fall into one of three traps:

1. Ignore it and hope it goes away.

2. Panic and pay it off recklessly, hurting cash flow.

3. Keep borrowing without a plan, making the problem worse.

The truth is simple: **Debt doesn't have to be a trap. It can be a tool—but only when you manage it intentionally.** When you know where every dollar is going and attack debt strategically, it stops being a burden and starts being a lever for growth.

The 3 Pillars to Mastering Debt

1. Make Every Dollar Work

Before you can pay down debt effectively, you need to see your cash clearly. This is about more than tracking income and expenses, it's about **designating every dollar a purpose**.

Set up dedicated accounts for:

- **Profit** – Your reward for running the business. Even a small profit, consistently allocated, builds confidence and stability.

- **Owner's Pay** – Make sure you're paying yourself before everyone else. This protects your personal finances and keeps motivation high.

- **Taxes** – Pay taxes consistently so they don't sneak up on you.

- **Operating Expenses** – Cover the cost of running the business without cutting corners.

- **Debt Repayment** – Make debt a predictable part of your monthly plan, like rent or utilities.

Think of your money like a pie. Before you spend on anything else, slice out pieces for these accounts. By giving debt its own slice, you **stop treating repayment as "optional"** and make progress automatic.

2. Snowball vs. Avalanche

Once you've locked your cash flow, it's time to **attack debt strategically**. There are two proven methods:

Snowball Method:

- Focus on the **smallest debts first** while making minimum payments on larger ones.

- Each debt you eliminate frees up extra cash and creates momentum.

- Psychologically, it feels amazing to cross items off your list, like clearing obstacles in your path.

Avalanche Method:

- Focus on debts with the **highest interest rates first**.

- This saves you the most money over time because interest is the sneaky "profit killer" on debts.

- Progress may feel slower, but mathematically, it costs you less overall.

Practical Tip: Take **50% of your profits** (after allocations) and put it toward debt repayment. If your profit account grows to $4,000, allocate $2,000 directly to debt. This extra push accelerates the payoff and gives you breathing room.

Think of it like this: debt is a mountain, and every extra dollar is a stepping stone. The more stones you place strategically, the faster you climb.

3. Strategic Growth

Once your debts are under control, growth becomes possible without gambling your cash. Borrow only when it's **intentional and integrated**:

- Integrate debt payments into your **monthly operating budget**. Don't let repayment surprise you.

- Treat borrowing like a **tool**, not a crutch. A loan for equipment that increases revenue makes sense—but a loan just to cover a shortfall in payroll does not.

- Continue focusing on **profit, not just revenue**. Revenue growth is exciting, but if profits don't grow, debt will quietly eat away at it.

Visualize debt as a lever. The right debt, paid strategically, lifts your business to new heights. The wrong debt weighs it down. Master the difference, and growth is no longer risky, it's predictable.

Real Client Transformation

Meet **Emma**, a small business owner who came to us struggling with debt and stagnant growth:

Emma's Business Before:

- Revenue: $40,000/month

- Operating Expenses: $35,000/month

- Net Profit: $2,000/month

- Credit Card Debt: $20,000

- Stress Level: High

The Problem:

- Unchecked expenses were quietly draining $5,000/month.

- Debt payments were inconsistent, causing interest to pile up.

- Even though revenue was decent, profits barely covered payroll and other obligations.

Step 1: Cash Flow Control

- Set up dedicated accounts for **Profit, Owner's Pay, Taxes, Operating Expenses, and Debt Repayment.**

- Allocated $4,000/month to profit first, which included a **$2,000 earmark for accelerated debt repayment.**

Step 2: Debt Paydown Strategy

- Emma chose a **combination of snowball and avalanche** methods:

    - Paid off her **smallest $3,000 debt first** to gain momentum.

    - Focused next on the **highest interest $10,000 credit card** to save on interest costs.

Step 3: Strategic Growth

- Stopped spending on unnecessary subscriptions and an underused office.

- Continued to grow revenue, but now **with profit and debt in mind**, ensuring every dollar worked harder.

Emma's Business After 90 Days:

- Revenue: $40,000/month (same, steady growth)

- Operating Expenses: $30,000/month (plugged $5,000 leaks)

- Net Profit: $6,000/month (tripled!)

- Credit Card Debt: $12,000 (paid $8,000 strategically)

- Stress Level: Low

- Growth Strategy: Strategic and predictable

The Result

By prioritizing profit allocation and using 50% of profits to accelerate debt repayment, Emma reduced her debt by **40% in just three months**. At the same time, by plugging leaks and controlling cash flow, her net profit **tripled**.

This transformation shows that it's not about revenue alone, it's about **making profits predictable, debt manageable, and growth strategic**.

Your Next Step

1. **Lock in your profits:** Set up accounts and allocate revenue first.

2. **Map your debt:** List all debts, interest rates, and minimum payments.

3. **Pick a paydown strategy:** Snowball, avalanche, or a mix.

4. **Commit 50% of profits to debt:** Accelerate repayment while keeping cash flow healthy.

5. **Grow with discipline:** Borrow only strategically and keep profit in mind.

Scaling without a plan is like building IKEA furniture without instructions, you *might* get it done, but it will be messy and stressful.

With these three pillars, you can outsmart debt, crush growth goals, and build lasting financial success, without losing sleep.

Closing Summary

Mastering debt isn't about avoiding risk or borrowing blindly, it's about **taking control of your cash flow and using debt strategically**. This gives you a clear roadmap to turn debt from a financial headache into a growth engine, **without losing sight of the main goal: profits, profits, profits**.

When you **allocate profits first, map out debts, and commit to a strategic repayment plan**, you stop guessing and start building a business that doesn't just grow, it thrives. Think of it like a houseplant: consistent care, the right resources, and a clear plan make it flourish.

Scaling without a solid profit and debt plan? That's like trying to build IKEA furniture without that tiny Allen wrench you can't find.

With the right system, mindset, and a little financial discipline, you can:

- **Outsmart debt** with a strategy that works for your business.

- **Accelerate growth** while keeping cash flow healthy.

- **Build lasting financial success** without losing sleep or sanity.

You've seen how **plugging leaks, allocating profits, and paying down debt strategically** transforms a business. Now it's time to take that foundation and **Sustain & Gain**—building a system that keeps your business thriving for the long haul.

FREE GIFT:
The Debt Freedom Snapshot

Crush debt without suffocating your cash flow. Most people attack debt blindly. This one-page snapshot fixes that. You'll see which debt is actually hurting you, where interest is quietly killing your profit, and the fastest win you can make this week to create momentum. No spreadsheets. No math. No shame. Just a simple plan that beats debt and keeps cash flowing.

Grab it at <u>findmyhiddenprofits.com/tools</u> or scan the QR code if you believe shortcuts are a sign of intelligence.

Chapter 9:
Escape Yesterday's Numbers — Unleash Your Power for Explosive Growth

Financial blind spots keep you stuck in reaction mode. Lack of visibility leads to decisions that can bury you in debt, but simple shifts in cash timing can change everything.

But blind spots aren't the only problem. Another major trap is **relying on yesterday's numbers to make today's decisions.**

Rearview Mirror Accounting

Ditra, a savvy CEO of an ed-tech company, watched her expenses pile up. Instead of helping her find profit-saving opportunities, her accountant just filed taxes. No forecasting. No planning. No strategy.

It was like they were speaking different languages.

By the time the numbers revealed trouble, it was already too late. Expenses had ballooned, margins had thinned, and no one had raised the flag soon enough to change course.

Here's the trap: too many business owners are told they're on track based on last year's numbers. But last year's numbers don't reflect today's reality. You've raised prices. You've hired. You've made strategic moves. Yet your reporting hasn't caught up, so it paints a picture of a business that no longer exists.

Ditra's story isn't unique. Most business owners receive reports that explain the past but do nothing to prepare them for the future.

Forward-Facing Financial Insight

We previous discussed fixing blind spots, now it's about getting your eyes on the road ahead.

Let me introduce you to my little friend…**The Cash Compass**.

This works because it doesn't just track what already happened, it helps you forecast, budget, and measure performance in real time.

Instead of waiting until tax season to find out what went wrong, you'll know where you stand today and what's coming tomorrow.

This shift—from rearview mirror accounting to forward-facing financial insight—is the key to growth.

Cash Compass

You don't need complex models to escape yesterday's numbers. Start small, create a **Cash Compass:**

- **List your top 5–10 recurring expenses.**
- **Project them out for the next 3 months.**
- **Overlay your expected revenue for the same period.**

And then, follow the money.

Even a basic forecast like this gives you a head start. You'll see cash gaps before they arrive, and you'll be able to make decisions with clarity instead of panic.

It's not about predicting the future perfectly, it's about preparing for it.

Ditra's Turnaround

Ditra eventually stopped waiting for her accountant's permission and hired a strategic advisor who used forecasting, budgeting, and performance reviews. Within months, her profitability rebounded.

She felt in control again.

Her stress went down. Her team's confidence went up. And she finally had the momentum to grow without fear.

That's what happens when you stop driving with the rearview mirror and start using a dashboard.

Closing Summary

Looking backward shows you what went wrong (like realizing sushi from a gas station was a mistake!). A simple Cash Compass helps you look ahead, but that's only the first step. Numbers can show you where you've been and even hint at where you're going, but they can't tell you what move to make next.

Because here's the truth: visibility without guidance still leaves you guessing.

In the next chapter, you'll discover how **Strategic Financial Guidance** bridges that gap. It's the missing piece that turns raw data into confident decisions, so you can stop second-guessing and start leading with clarity, strategy, and control.

FREE GIFT:
The Cash Compass Forecast Sheet

Stop running your business in the rearview mirror. This simple tool shows you the next 30–90 days, what cash is coming in, what bills are coming up, and whether you're heading toward a **cash** gap or a **cash** cushion. No formulas. No spreadsheets. Just instant visibility so you can make the right move before you need it.

Grab yours at findmyhiddenprofits.com/tools or scan the QR code because efficiency looks good on you.

Chapter 10:
Financial Guidance — From Blind Decisions to a Sure Win

In the last chapter, you learned how yesterday's numbers can keep you stuck in the past, and how building a forward-looking Cash Compass can give you visibility into where you're headed.

But visibility alone isn't enough. Even with the best dashboard, you still need **guidance**, someone to help you read the gauges, interpret the patterns, and decide what to do next. Because here's the truth: numbers don't make decisions. Leaders do.

Flying Blind in the Maze of Decisions

There's a deep emotional cost when your financial partner is focused on compliance and isn't comfortable providing real guidance.

- Every hiring choice feels like a gamble.

- Every pricing move feels like a shot in the dark.

- Every growth decision keeps you up at night, wondering if you're about to make a costly mistake.

And when the gamble doesn't pay off? You're left carrying the weight of that mistake, wondering if you should even play at all, because the rules feel impossible to figure out.

It's exhausting. And it's not because you're bad at business. It's because you're being forced to navigate the maze of decisions blindfolded.

Strategic Financial Guidance

The next piece of the **Cash Confidence Blueprint** is **Strategic Financial Guidance**, turning numbers into clarity and clarity into confident action.

It's not about more spreadsheets. It's about connecting your financial data to the decisions that matter most, so you can make bold moves with confidence instead of fear.

Now imagine having a strategic advisor who can look ahead, analyze trends, and guide you with clear options and recommendations. Someone who doesn't just file your paperwork, but helps you forecast your future.

Someone who's actually invested in helping you succeed.

With the right guidance, you'll:

- See the ripple effects of each decision before you make it.
- Know whether a big investment supports your goals, or puts them at risk.
- Have a trusted sounding board who helps you weigh the what-ifs and choose the smartest path forward.

This is how you shift from guessing to leading.

CPG = Cash-Profit-Growth

While nothing replaces having a true financial partner in your corner, here's a simple filter you can use right now to bring clarity to your next big decision. Before you act, ask three questions:

- **Cash** — How will this impact my cash in the next 90 days?
- **Profit** — How will this affect my margins this year?
- **Growth** — Does this move align with my long-term goals?

Even this quick filter gives you more clarity than relying on gut feelings alone. It forces you to connect financial impact to real-world decisions, with no MBA or a 40-page report.

Chris's Story

Chris, a software CEO, faced this exact challenge. He runs a growing software company. When the opportunity arose to expand his operations, he turned to his accountant for advice on financing the move. Instead of actionable insights or meaningful financial analysis, he was handed more spreadsheets, but no strategy. Chris was left guessing. He knew his product and market inside and out, but when it came to the financial side of this decision, he felt alone.

Overwhelmed, Chris froze. He avoided making the decision altogether.

Then came the sleepless nights, wondering if he was missing out on something big, afraid of making a costly mistake.

Eventually, Chris realized he didn't need more spreadsheets, he needed a sounding board. Everything changed when he brought on a strategic advisor. Instead of just reports, he got guidance: "Here's how this decision will affect your cash, your profit, and your growth." Within months, Chris made the leap confidently, and the expansion paid off.

You Deserve Better Than Blindfolded Decision-Making

Making big decisions without strategic financial support is like navigating a maze blindfolded, you're bound to hit walls, dead ends, and costly mistakes. The stress, uncertainty, and what-ifs don't just hurt your bottom line. They chip away at your confidence as a leader.

But it doesn't have to be this way. When you have the right financial guidance, someone who not only understands your numbers but helps you apply them in strategic, forward-looking ways, you stop guessing. You start leading. You grow with intention. You act with confidence.

Closing Summary

You shouldn't have to run your business with a blindfold on. Numbers alone won't guide you. Spreadsheets won't comfort you at 2 am. They're not proof that you're bad with money. They're just proof you've been juggling flaming batons—alone—and somehow still trying to smile through it. ¯_(ツ)_/¯

You need clarity, strategy, and someone in your corner who helps you connect the dots, so you stop second-guessing and start leading with confidence. And suddenly, your business isn't running you, you've got the wheel, GPS dialed in, no U-turns required.

In the next chapter, you'll see the real cost of missed opportunities, and how hesitation or lack of guidance can quietly drain your business. You'll discover a simple, actionable approach called **Name It, Claim It**, and learn how to reclaim just **one opportunity** that's holding back your growth.

FREE GIFT:
The CPG Decision Filter

Make your next big move with confidence, not guesswork. Most owners hire, fire, invest, or expand blind…and hope for the best. This 3-question filter fixes that fast. In under a minute, you'll see exactly how any decision impacts your Cash (next 90 days), Profit (this year), and Growth (long-term). No spreadsheets. No overthinking. No expensive mistakes.

Hop over to <u>findmyhiddenprofits.com/tools</u>
or scan the QR code if your thumbs need a break.

Chapter 11:
What Could Have Been — The Cost of Missed Opportunity

In the last chapter, we discussed how making major financial decisions without clear guidance leaves you guessing and stressed, like navigating a maze blindfolded.

Now, imagine the opportunities you might have missed.

The Hidden Cost of Missed Opportunities

Every time you hesitate because you don't have clarity, you risk losing momentum. Every time your accountant gives you a spreadsheet instead of a strategy, opportunities slip through the cracks.

And those missed opportunities don't just cost money. They cost:

- **Time** you can't get back.
- **Confidence** that gets chipped away with every what-if.
- **Growth** that stalls while you tread water.

The emotional weight of what could have been is heavy, because deep down, you know things could have been easier, smarter, faster with the right support.

Name It, Claim It

Opportunities don't vanish by chance, they vanish when no one names them. With the **Cash-Profit-Growth** from our last chapter, and the right strategic guidance, you don't just see what's happening; you see what's possible.

That means regular check-ins that ask:

- Where are we overspending?

- Where could we restructure or renegotiate?

- What tax-saving moves are we missing?

- Where's the hidden capacity for growth?

This isn't about tracking numbers. It's about turning numbers into conversations — conversations that reveal the opportunities you can name… and claim.

Reclaim Just One Opportunity

You don't need to overhaul your entire business to start. Choose one area where you suspect money is leaking or momentum is stalling. For example:

- **Debt**: Ask your bank about refinancing or restructuring one high-interest loan.

- **Vendors**: Negotiate better terms with just one key supplier.

- **Subscriptions**: Cancel or downgrade one recurring expense that no longer serves you.

Reclaiming even a single opportunity like this gives you proof you can turn setbacks into wins.

Daryl's Story

Take Daryl, for example. His construction company was paying high interest on loans because he didn't know how to restructure debt properly. His accountant didn't notice the warning signs of his debt situation and didn't suggest any options for improvement. They just kept tracking, tracking, tracking… and nearly tracked him all the way toward bankruptcy.

It was only after Daryl sought external advice he realized the real cost—deals missed, growth delayed, momentum lost. His business wasn't moving forward; it was quietly grinding to a halt.

But with the right financial guidance, Daryl turned things around. He restructured his debt, freed up cash flow, and reignited growth. What felt like a dead end became a turning point, one that put him back in control and on the path to building his business stronger than before.

That's the power of spotting and reclaiming missed opportunities before they sink you.

With strategic guidance, you can turn what feels like setbacks into your greatest comeback.

Closing Summary

Missed opportunities hurt, we've all got a few. They leave dents in your confidence and dings in your bank account. But they don't have to define your story.

Even small actions, like reclaiming just one opportunity, can prove that setbacks aren't permanent. They show you that with clarity and the right guidance, you can turn hesitation into momentum and start making decisions that actually grow your business.

FREE GIFT:
The Hidden Opportunity Roadmap

Stop leaking money like a rookie. This roadmap shows you one move
you can make THIS WEEK to reclaim cash, cut a cost, renegotiate a
vendor, or kill an expense that's robbing you blind. 5 minutes.
One win. Proof you're no longer leaving money on the table.
No overwhelm. No spreadsheets. Just one clear win that
proves you're back in control.

Get it at findmyhiddenprofits.com/tools or scan the QR code –
your future self did, and is very impressed!

Chapter 12:
Long-Term Success Starts Here–Create a Business That Fuels Your Life

Most business owners are rebels. You started by breaking rules, hustling hard, and doing things your way, and that early energy rewarded risk-taking. But what got you here won't get you there.

Starting on Wall Street before moving into entrepreneurship, I quickly noticed how differently most business owners are conditioned compared to the financial discipline I saw in big companies.

That early, frenetic energy of starting something new is often a break from bureaucracy; it's a way to break the rules, but there is a reason larger companies tend to outlive small businesses. It's because the big companies follow rules.

Without a sustainable system, your business can grow chaotically, leaving you reacting to stress, market swings, and unexpected expenses. Growth without structure isn't freedom, it's firefighting in slow motion.

I'd argue that deferring on sustainability (or stability) is one of the biggest mistakes in a typical business owner's belief system.

Sustain & Gain

Sustainability is the cornerstone of long-term success, and this 'pay yourself first' system builds it into your business from day one. And when I'm speaking with business owners, or dropping in on social media, this word, sustainability, is usually brushed aside as a nice-to-have or someday-maybe priority.

By focusing on profit and maintaining structured allocations, you create a resilient financial system that can weather economic downturns, market fluctuations, and unexpected expenses.

This sustainable approach allows you to plan for growth without constantly feeling like you're treading water. As your business becomes more profitable, you'll gain the freedom to reinvest, expand, or take profits out for personal use, all while maintaining a balanced, controlled financial system.

What's most powerful about this approach is that it isn't just a short-term fix, it's a long-term strategy. By building reserves and creating predictable cash flow, you're setting yourself up to make smarter decisions, even as emergencies and changing conditions appear.

Over time, the system becomes ingrained in your business's DNA, making it easier to scale, manage debt, and plan for the future. Rather than reacting to financial stress, you're proactively building a business that works for you, creating space for both personal and professional growth.

Plan To Win

Don't just hope for growth, decide what bold success looks like for the next 12 months.

1. **Set Bold Goals:** Review your business goals for the next 12 months. Ask yourself: are you pushing far enough, or holding

back because of past setbacks? Picture having a trusted system to test ideas confidently—what moves would you make?

2. **Define Profit Targets**: Get real about profit: what number would make you feel secure and in control?

3. **Profits On Lock**: Grab your profit allocations and map out exactly how much you need to set aside each quarter to hit those goals.

Write it down. Seeing it on paper turns ambition into action, and action into results.

Closing Summary

Building a sustainable business isn't just about surviving, it's about creating a solid foundation that can handle growth, curveballs, and sometimes chaotic weeks.

Smart financial systems protect your business from uncertainty and empower you to dream bigger and take bold, confident steps. Sustainability is the secret sauce that turns your vision into a thriving reality, weekends off included.

You've seen how this approach shifts you from reactive firefighting to proactive leadership. Next up, meet Jennifer—a business owner just like you—who went from barely breaking even to unlocking **10x profits** and true financial control. Her ah-ha moment? Real change doesn't come from working harder or chasing more sales, but from applying smart profit strategies to the business you already have.

Get ready for the roadmap that actually turned Jennifer's business— and sanity—around. GPS included.

FREE GIFT:
The 12-Month Plan-to-Win Blueprint

Hope doesn't scale. Plans do. This one-page blueprint locks in clarity on profit, reserves, and growth. In minutes, you'll define your top 3 goals, your sleep-at-night profit number, and exactly what to set aside each quarter, plus a quick Sustainability Score to make sure your plan actually works. No spreadsheets. No guessing. Just a plan you can follow all year.

Download at findmyhiddenprofits.com/tools or scan the QR code if your relationship with manual typing is complicated.

Chapter 13:

From Barely Breaking Even to 10x Profits–Jennifer's Life Changing Moment

Jennifer knew how to hustle. A seasoned attorney who built a thriving title and escrow agency from scratch, Jennifer scaled it to nearly $1 million in annual revenue. From the outside, it looked like a winning business, but behind the scenes, something didn't add up.

Every month, after covering payroll, office expenses, and vendor bills, she was left with a razor-thin margin. Just $18,000 in profit for the year. That's a tough number when you realize she was working 60+ hour weeks, juggling a team, and carrying a $25,000 credit card balance that only seemed to grow. She wasn't failing. But she wasn't winning either.

> *"I was doing all the right things… or so I thought. But no matter how hard I worked, there just wasn't enough left over. I couldn't pay myself consistently. I felt like I was one bad month away from disaster."*

Her wake-up call came when she realized: she'd earned nearly $1 million that year and couldn't afford to take a vacation or pay herself with any consistency.

Jennifer knew she needed help, not just with bookkeeping or taxes, but with actually understanding her business finances in a way that gave her clarity, control, and direction.

What followed changed everything.

10X Profits

The shift came when Jennifer implemented the **Cash Confidence Blueprint**: a step-by-step approach to identify hidden leaks, capture missed opportunities, optimize operations, and take control of cash flow. Instead of hustling harder, she worked smarter with the business she already had.

Step One: Plug the Cash Leaks

The first step was an honest look at where the money was going. Together, we conducted a deep-dive. What we found surprised even Jennifer: **$9,500 in unnecessary expenses per month**. By cutting these, Jennifer freed up **$114,000 per year**—without adding a single new client.

Step Two: Small Price Tweaks, Big Impact

Next, we examined pricing. By adjusting undercharged administrative fees and closing costs, Jennifer added **another $1,200/month to her bottom line**. That's **$14,400 a year**, from capturing value she was already delivering. Small wins. Big difference.

Step Three: Right-Sizing Her Team and Vendors

Jennifer was also carrying the cost of an underperforming team member, someone she liked, but who wasn't delivering. Letting go of an underperforming salesperson saved **$50,000/year.** Next, she renegotiated vendor contracts, cut overlap, and added another **$2,500/month**. These operational changes alone added **$80,000/ year in profit**.

Step Four: Cash Flow Control

This tackled the biggest source of stress: unpredictable cash flow. With debt restructuring, vendor negotiations, and quarterly tax planning, we turned unpredictable cash flow into a predictable, stress-free system.

These weren't just financial shifts, they gave Jennifer peace of mind and put her back in the driver's seat of her business.

The Results: 10X Profit + Peace

Let's zoom out.

Before:

- Revenue: $80,000/month
- Profit: $1,500/month ($18,000/year)
- Stress level: High

After:

- Revenue: $81,200/month (a modest 1.5% increase)
- Profit: $16,683/month ($199,000/year)
- Stress level: Low; sleeps like a baby

Jennifer now pays herself $10,000/month, her office rent is manageable, and the $25,000 credit card balance is disappearing—with no extra hustle.

> *"This changed everything for me," Jennifer says. "I thought I had to make more money to be more profitable. But it turns out, I just needed to be smarter with the money I already had."*

Closing Summary

Jennifer's story is proof that profit isn't just for the lucky, the ultra-scaled math people, or those with a suspicious obsession with spreadsheets. It's possible—right now—with the business you already have.

She didn't hustle harder.

She didn't double her sales.

She didn't sell her soul to the algorithm.

She took **control.**

You don't need a bigger business. You need a better system.

One that finally pays *you* back, because last time we checked, you're not running a nonprofit. Real success isn't about chasing more revenue, it's about creating a business that gives more than it takes. Start applying this system today and watch your business finally pay you back.

In the next chapter, we'll move from **inspiration to implementation.** You'll learn how to set up your system, make profit non-negotiable, and turn your business into a true wealth engine, so it fuels the life you want, not just your work. Think of it as the bridge between financial awareness and financial empowerment.

Your journey from reactive stress to confident control continues—let's make it real.

FREE GIFT:
The 10x Profit Quick Audit

Jennifer didn't make more money, she found it. She pulled $181,000 out of the business she already had; you can too. The difference? She finally saw where the money was hiding. This 10-minute audit does the same. No spreadsheets, no math, no financial trauma. You'll spot the leaks draining profit, the fastest wins to fix this week, and the cash you can reclaim now.

Grab it here at <u>findmyhiddenprofits.com/tools</u> or scan the QR code for minimal effort, maximum upside.

Chapter 14:
The 90-Day Profit Plan – From Cash Chaos To Building Your Profit Machine

You've seen it firsthand: revenue doesn't equal freedom. Even solid sales can leave you stuck in a reactive financial fog, wondering, *"Where did all the money go?"* Jennifer's story proves it—she went from $18K/year profit to nearly $200K/year, without working harder, just by applying a system.

Now it's your turn. In the next 90 days, you can stop chasing cash and start creating predictable profit, a system that works even when you're not looking. No luck. No guesswork. Just a clear, step-by-step plan to take control, reclaim your freedom, and grow your business into a true wealth engine.

Why Now Matters

Profit isn't a spreadsheet line item, it's the fuel for your lifestyle, your freedom, and your future. The best time to start? Yesterday. The second-best time? Today. Every moment you delay is profit left on the table.

This is your rallying cry: implement, act, and lead. Not someday. Not next quarter. **Right now.**

Quick Wins to Kickstart Control

- **Open your bank accounts** – Profit, Taxes, Owner's Pay, Operating Expenses. Allocate money as it comes in.
- **Put profit on lock** – Even 1% counts. Start small, but start now.
- **Accountability and clarity** – Track, review, and adjust monthly.

Next, here is your 90-day roadmap to success.

Phase 1: Week 1–4 – Discover & Diagnose

Goal: Create a **Hidden Cash Flow Hit List**. This is a complete inventory of all the money flowing out of your business—both obvious and sneaky

Before you can start paying down debt and growing your business, you need to know exactly where your money is leaking. Most business owners focus on revenue, but unchecked expenses are the real profit killers.

Here's how to do it:

1. **Pull your last three months of expenses** – bank statements and credit card statements

2. **Break them down into categories:**
   a. Operating costs (rent, utilities, software, subscriptions)
   b. Employee and contractor costs
   c. Marketing and advertising
   d. Miscellaneous small expenses that add up

3. **Highlight the sneaky money drains** – recurring charges you forgot, services you don't use, and overpriced vendors.

4. **Ask the critical question for each expense:** *"Is this absolutely necessary right now to grow my business or keep it running smoothly?"*

Result: You now have a prioritized list of expenses to trim, reduce, or eliminate.

This is your **Hidden Cash Flow Hit List**—the foundation for freeing up money to pay down debt and fuel growth.

Quick Tip: Start with the "low-hanging fruit" – small recurring expenses you can stop right away. The savings may surprise you.

Phase 2: Week 5–8 – Fix & Optimize

Goal: Plug leaks, streamline operations, and increase efficiency.

Steps:

1. **Cut Costs Wisely** – Big wins first. Small cuts later.
2. **Boost Revenue Strategically** – Focus on high-margin products, upsells, and premium options.
3. **Accountability** – Track weekly, assign accountability.
4. **Adopt a Profit-First Mindset** – Protect profit before paying bills.

Mini Checklist:

- Top expense reductions implemented
- Revenue optimization plan in place
- Weekly accountability system established
- Profit-first allocations started

Result: Controlled costs, improved margins, and a business running predictably.

Phase 3: Week 9–12 – Predict & Scale

Goal: Turn your system into predictable, sustainable profit.

Steps:

1. **Double Down on What Works** – Keep profitable clients/products; ditch what drains resources.

2. **Maintain Cash Discipline** – Weekly and monthly reviews keep profit top of mind.

3. **Plan Growth Experiments** – Small, measurable tests: price tweaks, new offerings, efficiency gains.

Result: Predictable profit, smoother cash flow, and a repeatable system for growth without chaos.

Take Control Today

Profit doesn't happen by accident, it's designed. These 90 days are about action, discipline, and clarity. Start today. Track progress. Adjust as needed. By day 90, you'll no longer be chasing cash—you'll have a predictable profit that gives you freedom and control.

Your Next Actions:

- Set up Profit, Taxes, Owner's Pay, OPEX accounts

- Make your first allocation—even 1% counts

- Review numbers monthly

You don't have to do it alone. With guidance, your system won't just exist, it will **work for you, grow with you, and build the future you deserve**.

Let's crush these next 90 days.

You've got this. And I've got your back.

FREE GIFT:
The 90-Day Momentum Map

Predictable profit doesn't require more clients or more spreadsheets. It requires a plan you'll actually finish.

This one-page Momentum Map lays out a 12-week path to stabilize cash, cut chaos, and build real profit—fast. You'll get the 3 phases, the quick wins, and the weekly actions that keep momentum high and guesswork out. No fluff. No overwhelm. Just a clear 90-day plan that puts you back in control.

Grab it here at <u>findmyhiddenprofits.com/tools</u> or scan the QR code. Your next 90 days will change everything. **Start now.**

Chapter 15:
Profit Next™ — Building a Profit-to-Wealth Blueprint

By now, you've done a lot of thinking, reflecting, and, more importantly, acting.

You've looked at your numbers with fresh eyes. You've learned to prioritize profit and cash flow, not as an afterthought, but as a strategy.

You've started to unlearn the toxic myths around hustle, reinvesting everything, and waiting until "someday" to pay yourself. And maybe, for the first time, you can actually picture a business that serves *you*.

But here's the realization that hits next:

Profit First is the beginning. Not the destination.

To become profitable, you need **precision**.

Once your business is profitable…the real question becomes:

Now what?

Introducing Profit Next™

Profit Next™ is what happens *after* profitability.

It's the shift from running a profitable business to **designing a wealth engine**. From reacting to numbers… to commanding them. From asking *"Can I afford this?"* to *"Is this the smartest move for my future?"*

Profit Next™ goes beyond allocations and formulas. It aligns your business with your **life, wealth, and legacy goals**.

This is where you stop operating month-to-month, and start thinking like the CEO of your future.

How High-Performing Leaders Use Profit Next™

High performers don't stop at "extra cash in the bank."

They use Profit Next™ to:

- Build safety nets that actually feel safe
- Make growth decisions without second-guessing
- Pay themselves consistently *and* fund team and opportunity
- Turn profit into long-term, personal wealth

They don't ask, *"How do I survive growth?"*
They ask, *"How do I use growth to buy back time, freedom, and optionality?"*

That's the difference.

The Mistake Most Profitable Owners Make

Most business owners hit profitability and pause.

They pay themselves a little more. They breathe for a minute. They assume freedom is next.

But stress still shows up. Growth still feels risky. And taxes still feel like a surprise attack.

Because profit alone doesn't create freedom.

Design does.

Profit Next™ is about making your money intentional, so it supports the life you're building, not just the business you're running.

Closing Summary

Profit is a milestone. **Wealth is a system.**

Profit Next™ takes you from "this business works" to "this business works *for me*."

It's not about doing more. It's about making what you've already built work harder, smarter, and longer.

FREE GIFT:
The Profit-To-Wealth Roadmap

If you're already generating solid revenue and feel like you're this close, but something still isn't clicking…this is for you. This complimentary Profit-to-Wealth Roadmap is designed for business owners who need sharper moves. No pitch deck. No fluff. Just clarity.

In this session, we'll:

- Identify the 1–2 tweaks that unlock the biggest leverage in your business
- Map the fastest path from **revenue** to **profitability**
- Discover how to use **profit** to upgrade your **lifestyle, build wealth, or fund your legacy**

Grab your spot here <u>findmyhiddenprofits.com/profit-to-wealth</u> or scan the QR code.

Profit First gets you out of the danger zone.
Profit Next™ decides what you do with the win.

Acknowledgements

Writing this book has been one of the most rewarding—and humbling—experiences of my life. It would not have been possible without the encouragement, insight, and support of so many incredible people.

Family

To my husband, **Peter**, thank you for being my comic relief when things get tough.

To my daughter, **Ava**, thank you for the honor of being your mom in this lifetime.

To my mother, **Gail**, thank you for all of the 7 am phone calls.

To my father, **Guy**, thank you for the continued guidance from the other side.

To the rest of my family - thank you for all of your continued love and support. The small things matter.

Friends

To my close friends who cheered me on and asked, "How's the book coming?" - thank you for keeping me motivated when I needed it most. Your enthusiasm reminded me why this work matters.

Team

To my incredible team—thank you for being the steady engine behind this work. Your dedication, attention to detail, and commitment to excellence allowed me to stay focused on writing and sharing this message.

A special thank-you to **Cyan Waymel-LeStat** for taking care of my business life and to **Jennifer Kennedy** for taking care of my personal life. I'm so grateful to have you as support.

Business Owners and Contributors

Writing this book would not have been possible without the generous insights and experiences shared by the many individuals I had the privilege of interviewing. Each conversation added depth, clarity, and perspective to the ideas throughout these pages.

I'm especially grateful to the following business owners and professionals who allowed me to share their stories, challenges, and triumphs:

- Allan Langer, CEO of The 7 Secrets Sales Academy
- Amanda Kaufman, CEO of Kaufman Services
- Amberly Lago, CEO of Inspired Living
- Anthony Luna, CEO of Coastline Equity
- Ariel Madrid Tolentino, CEO of Masterminds Institute
- Arlene Washburn, CEO of AVConnexions
- Ben Bonnell, Founder of Morgan Benjamin Search Group
- Brandon Martini, Founder of Stratus Financial
- Brian Traichel, Founder of Find A Business Pro!
- Catherine B. Roy, CEO of Catherine B. Roy LLC
- Charlie VanDerven, CEO of Social Advisors
- Chris Cayer, Founder of Speakers Phoenix Media
- Crystal Langdon, Founder of Crystal Clear Finances, Inc.
- David McSwain, CEO of McSwain Consulting
- Demetra Moore, Founder of Moore Out Of Life
- Diane Faulkner, Founder of Full Circle Press

- Ebert Grobler, Co-Founder of Ruby Search Solutions
- Emanuel Rose, CEO of Strategic eMarketing
- Eric LeGoff, Co-Founder of Evermore Global Advisors
- Eric Rozenberg, Founder of Event Business Formula
- Fei Wu, Founder of Feisworld Media
- Gigi Robinson, Founder of Hey It's Gigi
- Greg Mester, Founder of 5amMesterScrum
- Greg Stephens, Founder of Alignment Resources
- Jaiden Houston, CEO of Jay Restorations
- Jay Prock, Founder of Tidewater Staffing
- Joe Infante, Founder of Compass Left
- Joni Chan, Founder of Responsible Design Works
- Kelsey Nicole Nelson, Founder of Kelsey Nicole Nelson Media
- Kris Garlewicz, Founder of Prosperifi
- Laura Fredricks, CEO of The Ask
- Lisa Nicholls, Founder of Tira! Strategies
- Lisa Panarello, Founder of Careers Advance
- Lisa Steele, Founder of Fresh Eggs Daily
- Lynn Greenberg, CEO of Pivt
- Mallika Malhotra, Founder of The Brand CEO
- Mark X. Cronin, Co-Founder of John's Crazy Socks
- Marshall Atkinson, Founder of Marshall Atkinson Consulting
- Matt Schwartz, Founder of MJS Executive Search
- Megan Bond, Founder of MB Marketing
- Melissa Kelii, CEO of Honeycomb Bond LLC
- Michael Buzinski, CEO of Buzzworthy Marketing
- Michael Merida, Founder of Rockin' Roots
- Mike Michalowicz, Co-Founder & Author of Profit First
- Natasha Fallico, Founder of OncoScript
- Nathalie Gregg, CEO of Nathalie Gregg
- Nicholas Pope, Co-Founder of Washington Avenue Advisors
- Quinn Lemley, CEO of Quinn Lemley
- Dr. Ravi Iyer, CEO of IR Focal Point
- Robyn Crane, CEO of Robyn Crane, Inc.
- Ron Saharyan, Co-Founder of Profit First Professionals

- Shep Hyken, Founder of Shepard Presentations, Inc.
- Stefano Iaboni, Founder of Smile Solution, LLC
- Stephen Steers, Founder of Steers Consulting Group
- Steve Nudelberg, Founder of On The Ball Ventures
- Taren Sartler, Founder of Tick Tock It's About Time LLC
- Tina Unrue, CEO of Selfish Mama LLC
- Travis Baldwin, CEO of Elemental Eco Holdings, Inc.
- Ty Bennett, CEO of Ty Bennett
- Wayde Elliott - CEO of StoreIt.com
- Yvonne DiVita, CEO of Master Book Builders

Your willingness to be open, candid, and real has made this book a valuable resource for others on a similar path.

To my early readers, advisors, and clients—you helped shape the direction of this book with your feedback and encouragement. Thank you for believing in the mission behind it.

About the Author

Debra Angilletta is a seasoned business finance consultant and Master Certified Profit First Advisor with over 30 years of experience. She helps high-performing business owners take control of their cash flow, grow profits, and scale with confidence. A former Wall Street professional turned trusted advisor, she brings a rare mix of strategic insight and real-world practicality to business finances.

Debra specializes in service-based businesses, earning solid revenue, but still feeling stuck when it comes to money. What sets her apart? **Most financial planners never see your P&L. Tax pros aren't thinking long-term. Accountants don't focus on strategy.** Debra does. She's done financial planning, understands tax, and reads your numbers like a second language—connecting it all into one clear, profit-driving strategy.

Through her advisory work, she helps high-performance leaders uncover hidden profit, build sustainable systems, and make confident, data-backed decisions. An early adopter of Profit First, Debra has guided hundreds of businesses through it, but for her, Profit First is the beginning. Her signature framework, *Profit Next*™, turns simple allocation into a full financial strategy, so you build a business that pays you back in income, clarity, and long-term wealth.

When she's not advising clients or speaking on financial empowerment, you'll find her at 6 am Pilates, soaking up beach days with her daughter, flying through audiobooks at 2x speed, enjoying family dinners, laughing with friends, and cheering on her husband's NY team, savoring the small moments that turn everyday life into something unforgettable.

Learn more at findmyhiddenprofits.com.